OUR LIVING PLANET

Oceans

BLACKBIRCH®
PRESS

THOMSON
GALE

San Diego • Detroit • New York • San Francisco • Cleveland
New Haven, Conn. • Waterville, Maine • London • Munich

For more information, contact
The Gale Group, Inc.
27500 Drake Rd.
Farmington Hills, MI 48331-3535
Or you can visit our Internet site at http://www.gale.com

Adapted by A S Publishing from
Los Océanos © Parramon Ediciones S.A. 1996

Editor: Rosa Fragua
Text: Marta Serrano
Illustrations: Miquel Ferrón, Miriam Ferrón, Lidia Di Blasi
Design: Beatriz Seoane
Layout: Josep Guasch
Production: Rafael Marfil

LIBRARY OF CONGRESS CATALOGING-IN-PUBLICATION DATA

Serrano, Marta.
  Oceans / by Marta Serrano.
     v. cm. — (Living planet series)
  Includes index.
  Contents: Our watery planet —The ocean depths — Waves and tides — Life in the oceans — Coral reefs.
   ISBN 1-56711-669-8 (hbk. : alk. paper)
   1. Ocean—Juvenile literature. 2. Oceanography —Juvenile literature.
   [1. Ocean.] I. Title. II. Series.
   GC21.5 .S46 2003
   551.46—dc21   2002009527

Printed in Spain
10 9 8 7 6 5 4 3 2 1

CONTENTS

OUR WATERY PLANET

In ancient times, people knew little about the oceans. People who fished did not dare to go far from the shore because of the stories people told of gods and monsters that lived in the seas. It took courage for sailors to travel across the oceans, but by the beginning of the twentieth century, most of the world's oceans had been mapped. Today, only the ocean deeps have yet to be fully explored.

In ancient Greek legend, the sirens lured sailors to death on the rocks. Ulysses put wax in the ears of the crew and had himself tied to the mast so that he could safely listen to their song.

The oceans contain enormous resources and have traditionally been a source of free food for anyone with a boat. Fish are rich in protein, fats, minerals, and vitamins, and fishing is a major industry. The oceans also contain salt and other minerals.

The world's oceans contain 97 percent of the water in the world. The other 3 percent is in glaciers, rivers, lakes, and underground streams. Together, all the water in the world is called the hydrosphere. The water on land, which usually does not contain salt, is constantly renewed through a process called the water cycle (below). The sun's heat evaporates water from the salty oceans and from the land. Plants also give off water vapor through their leaves in a process called transpiration. All this invisible water vapor is swept upward.

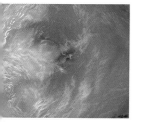

From space, the earth looks like a blue globe. The color comes from the water that covers over 70 percent of the planet's surface.

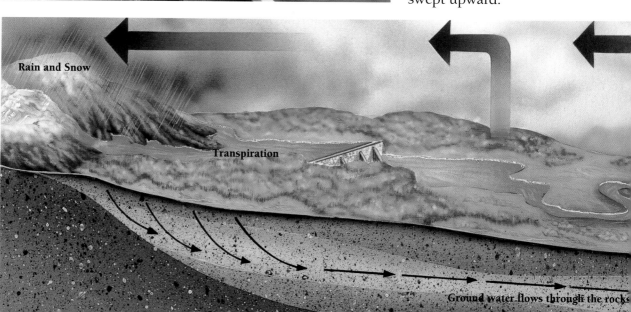

Rain and Snow

Transpiration

Ground water flows through the rocks

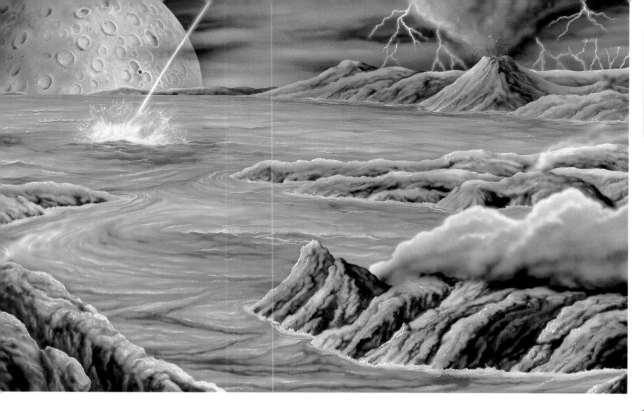

In the cool air high above the ground, the water vapor condenses into tiny water droplets. Billions of these droplets form clouds. Winds blow the clouds over the land and bring rain and snow. The rain flows into rivers or sinks into the ground. Then, either above or below ground, the water flows downhill to makes its way back to the oceans to complete one journey in the endless cycle.

As water makes its way back to the sea, it dissolves chemical substances called salts from the rocks. These salts end up in the oceans, which is why the sea is so salty. When water evaporates from the surface of the sea, the salt remains behind, which is why water on land is fresh, not salty, and we are able to drink it. Only saltwater fish and other sea creatures are able to tolerate seawater.

When the earth formed millions of years ago, it had a hot, molten surface (above). Volcanoes released water vapor into the air, and storms raged in the sky. Then, the surface slowly cooled, and rain began to fill hollows on the surface. It rained for millions of years, and this rain formed the seas and oceans.

The early seas were warmer than the seas are today, and it was in them that living things first appeared. The sea pro-tected the first living things against harmful ultraviolet rays from the sun. Ancient sea plants produced a gas called oxygen. A type of oxygen, called ozone, began to collect in an invisible layer high in the sky. This ozone layer blocked the sun's most dangerous rays and enabled the first animals to live on the land. Humans are still protected by the ozone layer.

The early seas were filled by rain from great storms. Many life forms evolved in the oceans, long before plants and animals were able to live on land.

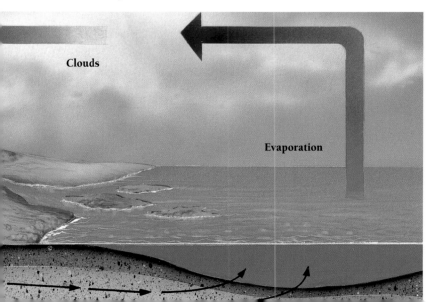

Clouds

Evaporation

THE OCEAN DEPTHS

People once thought that the ocean floor was a vast, flat plain. But scientists have discovered that it is as varied as land areas, with plains, mountain ranges, huge volcanoes, canyons, and even deeper trenches. The water in areas near land is relatively shallow. These areas are called continental shelves. They are flooded parts of the continents. The continental shelf off northwestern Europe extends about 186 miles (300 km) out to sea, but most shelves are narrower than this.

In some places, canyons cross the continental shelves. The shelves come to an end at the continental slope, which marks the edge of the continent. The continental slope plunges down to the ocean depths, called the abyss. The average depth of the abyssal plains is about 13,123 feet (4,000 m). These plains are covered by soft material called oozes that includes mud, clay, and the remains of dead sea creatures.

Many isolated volcanoes rise from the abyssal plains. Some of them, called seamounts, are completely submerged by water. Some reach the surface as islands. Ancient volcanoes with flat tops are called guyots. Guyots were probably volcanic islands that were worn down by the waves and then submerged beneath them.

Among the most impressive features of the sea

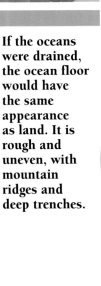

If the oceans were drained, the ocean floor would have the same appearance as land. It is rough and uneven, with mountain ridges and deep trenches.

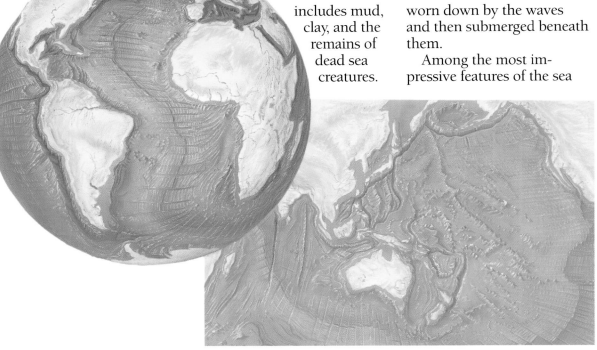

Guyot

Continental shelf

Abyssal plain

Oozes

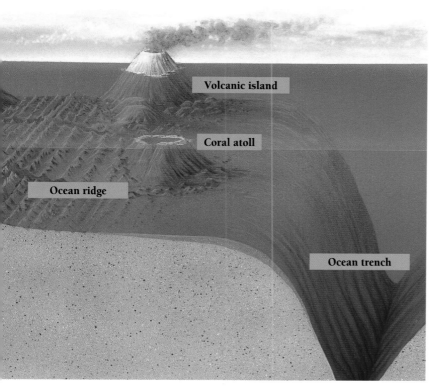

Volcanic island

Coral atoll

Ocean ridge

Ocean trench

seabed, with a total height of 33,481 feet (10,205 m). Only 13,796 feet (4,205 m) of the mountain appear above sea level.

By contrast, the oceans also contain deep trenches, some of which plunge down more than 6.2 miles (10 km) below sea level. Some of the deepest places in the oceans are shown on the map (right). Alongside many of the trenches are chains of volcanic islands.

floor are the ocean ridges. These ridges are the world's longest mountain ranges, although they are mostly hidden by seawater. Although their average height is only about 9,843 feet (3,000 m), some volcanic peaks break the surface as islands. Iceland lies on the Atlantic Ocean ridge, which runs the length of the ocean but surfaces only occasionally.

Sometimes, underwater volcanoes reach the surface in a series of spectacular

explosions (above left). For example, the island of Surtsey (above right) first appeared off Iceland in the North Atlantic Ocean in 1963. When the eruptions ceased by 1967, the island covered more than 1 square mile (2.6 sq km).

Volcanoes also created the islands that make up Hawaii in the North Pacific Ocean. Mauna Kea, a volcano on the largest island in Hawaii, is the world's highest mountain when measured from the

The oceans contain deep trenches. Alongside many of them are volcanoes, some of which are high enough to have become islands.

1 Mariana Trench 36,161 feet (11,022 m)
2 Aleutian Trench 25,663 feet (7,822 m)
3 Japan Trench 34,626 feet (10,554 m)
4 Philippine Trench 34,439 feet (10,497 m)
5 Chile Trench 26,411 feet (8,050 m)
6 Peru Trench 22,526 feet (6,866 m)
7 Central America Trench 21,857 feet (6,662 m)

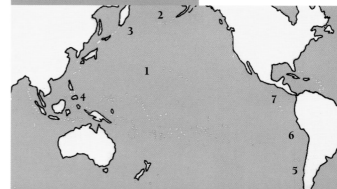

THE CHANGING OCEANS

Earth contains three large ocean basins and one smaller basin. They are the Pacific Ocean, which is the largest and covers about a third of the earth's surface; the Atlantic Ocean; the Indian Ocean; and the Arctic Ocean. All these oceans are interconnected.

Linked to the oceans are smaller areas called seas. The Mediterranean, Black, and Caribbean Seas, for example, are all arms of the Atlantic Ocean. The narrow Strait of Gibraltar, which is only 8.7 miles (14 km) wide, joins the Mediterranean Sea to the Atlantic Ocean. Another narrow waterway links the Black and Mediterranean Seas. The Caspian Sea, however, is completely surrounded by land, and many people regard it as the world's largest lake. But the Caspian Sea differs from most other large lakes because it contains salty water.

The positions of the continents and ocean basins have changed throughout the earth's history. Around 300 million years ago, the continents began to move together to form a single landmass. This landmass began to break up around 180 million years ago. By 60 million years ago, most of the landmasses were separated from each other. They continued to move a few inches a year, until they reached their present positions.

The continents and oceans were not always where they are now. They are moving all the time, edging slowly together or apart. A map of the world may once have looked like this.

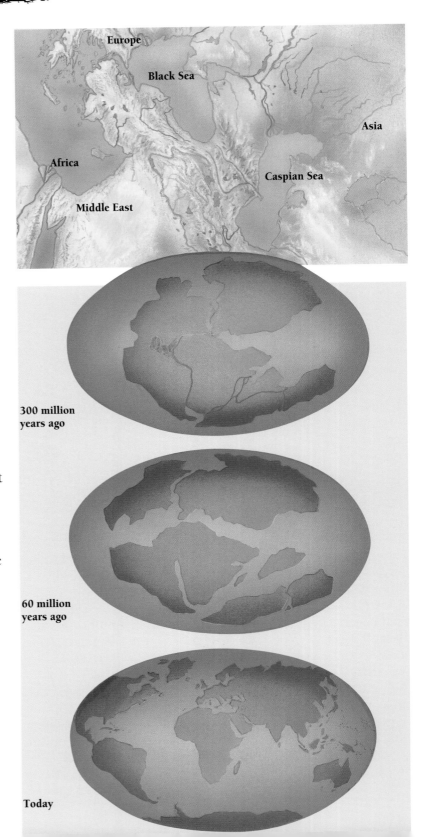

Europe
Black Sea
Asia
Africa
Caspian Sea
Middle East

300 million years ago

60 million years ago

Today

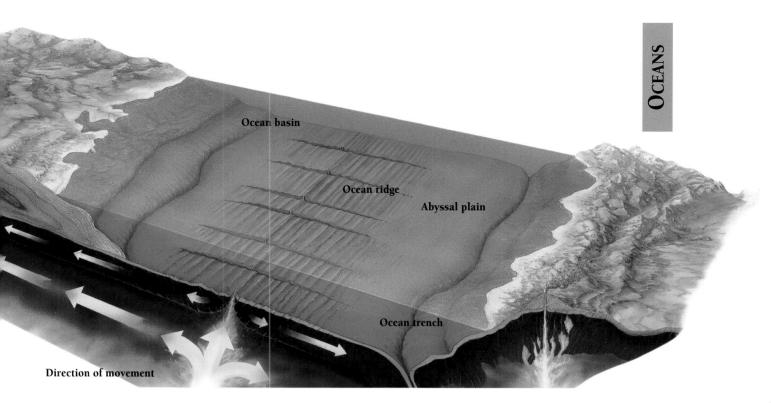

Ocean basin

Ocean ridge

Abyssal plain

Ocean trench

Direction of movement

The hard outer layers of the earth are split into huge blocks called plates. The plates are between 43.4 miles (70 km) and 62 miles (100 km) thick, but they are moved around by currents in the partly molten rocks beneath them. Along the ocean ridges, hot molten rock rises along a central trough, called a rift valley. The molten rock spreads out and pushes the plates apart. Molten rock plugs the gap made as the plates move apart. This molten rock hardens to form new rock. In this way, the ocean basins expand and the continents are pushed apart.

The earth is not getting any bigger, though, because the opposite happens along the ocean trenches. There, one plate is pushed down beneath another, and melts as it descends. Some of the molten rock rises through volcanoes that form on the surface above.

In some places, new oceans are being formed. The Red Sea, for example, is gradually widening as two plates move apart. The diagrams (below) show stages in the development of a new ocean. First, molten rock rises beneath a landmass along a central rift valley. Slowly, currents in the liquid rocks beneath the plates widen the rift valley. Finally, the sea floods into the central area and forms an ocean basin.

Today
In some places, continents are being pushed apart as new rock forms the bed of a new ocean and water flows in to fill the gap.

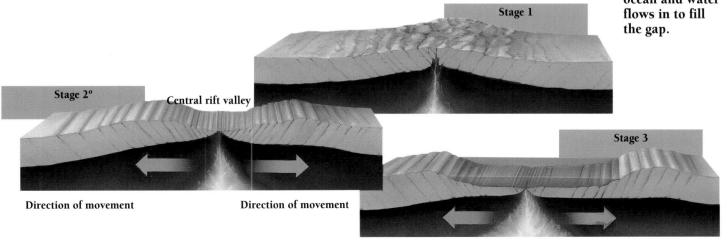

Stage 1

Stage 2°   Central rift valley

Direction of movement   Direction of movement

Stage 3

WAVES AND TIDES

Along the seashore, seawater is always on the move. Waves crash against cliffs or break gently along beaches, while tides change the water level. When the air is still, the sea is calm (below). When breezes blow across the water, they ruffle the surface of the water and create low waves. Strong winds create great turbulence that leads to high foam-topped waves (right).

From time to time, huge waves flood the land and cause devastation. They are caused by hurricanes or by underwater volcanic eruptions or earthquakes.

The height of waves depends on the wind's strength. In stormy weather, waves reach 39.4 feet (12 m) or more. The highest recorded wave in the open sea was 112 feet (34 m). It was measured during a severe storm in the Pacific Ocean. Waves that form in the open sea can travel long distances. This explains why waves can be seen along coasts when there is little or no wind.

The biggest waves that strike coasts are triggered by earthquakes under the sea or by volcanic eruptions. These great surges, which travel through the water at up to 496 miles per hour (800 km/h), are called tsunamis, a Japanese word. They are also called tidal waves, which is inaccurate because they are not caused by tides. Violent storms that coincide with high tides often cause terrible loss of life.

In open seas, waves move the water up and down but do not move it forward. Their movement is similar to shaking a rope that is tied to a tree. Waves are created, but the rope itself does not move forward. Only on coasts, where waves drag on the bottom, does the water actually move back and forth. When waves break, air bubbles mix with water to create white foam.

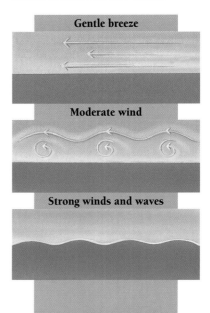

Gentle breeze

Moderate wind

Strong winds and waves

Twice every 24 hours and 50 minutes, the water level in the oceans rises and falls (right). These regular changes are called tides. They occur because the moon and, to a lesser extent, the sun exert a gravitational pull on the oceans. Because of this gravitational pull, the surface of the water on the side of the earth that faces the moon or sun is pulled away from the solid bulk of the earth, which forms a bulge. Another bulge in the opposite direction occurs on the far side of the earth. The bulges are the positions of the high tides. As the earth rotates, the bulges move around the planet.

Tides are low in partially enclosed seas, such as the Mediterranean. The highest tides occur when the rising water is funneled into narrow places such as river mouths.

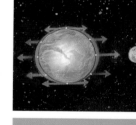

Tides are caused by the gravitational pull of the moon and sun on the oceans. The moon has a greater effect than the sun, because it is much nearer to the earth.

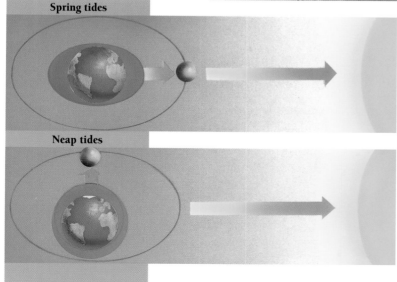

Spring tides

Neap tides

The highest and lowest tides, called spring tides, occur when the earth, moon, and sun are in a straight line. At that time, the gravitational pulls of the sun and moon are combined. Neap tides, when the difference between high and low tide is at its lowest, occur when the moon, sun, and earth form a right angle. This means that the gravitational pulls of the moon and the sun partly cancel each other out.

RIVERS IN THE OCEANS

People sometimes call ocean currents "rivers in the sea." Ocean currents move and mix vast amounts of water all over the planet. The world's main wind belts play a major part in the creation of surface currents. When winds blow constantly in the same direction, they push the surface waters in that direction. The direction in which currents flow, however, is altered slightly by the earth's rotation. Because of the spinning movement of the earth on its axis, ocean currents veer to the right of wind directions in the northern hemisphere and to the left in the southern hemisphere.

Cold currents move from the poles toward the equator, while warm currents flow from the tropics toward the poles. For these reasons, currents in the northern hemisphere tend to move in a clockwise direction, while those in the southern hemisphere move counterclockwise. The cold water that flows from the polar regions is dense, or heavy, so it sinks down and flows very slowly toward the equator along the ocean floor. This water replaces the warm water carried away from the equator by surface currents that flow over the top of the deeper water.

Warm surface currents affect the top 1,148 feet (350 m) of the oceans, while cold currents move in deeper water. When opposing currents meet, whirlpools may occur.

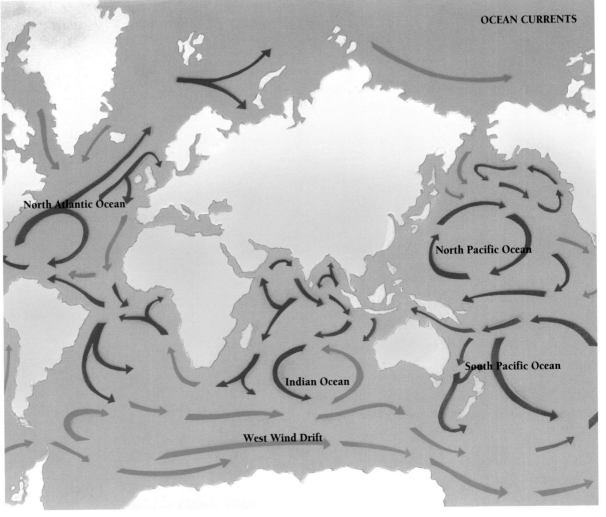

OCEAN CURRENTS

North Atlantic Ocean

North Pacific Ocean

Indian Ocean

South Pacific Ocean

West Wind Drift

Ocean currents carry warm water to polar regions and cold water to the hot tropics, so that polar regions do not become too cold or tropical regions too hot. Ocean currents also affect the climate of coastal regions. For example, the warm Gulf Stream flows from the Caribbean Sea across the North Atlantic Ocean. This current brings mild weather to the British Isles and Norway. Cold currents off the west coasts of southern Africa and South America chill areas on the shore.

Salinity (the saltiness of water) also affects currents. For example, the water in the Mediterranean Sea is saltier than that in the open Atlantic Ocean because of evaporation in the warm Mediterranean region. Salty

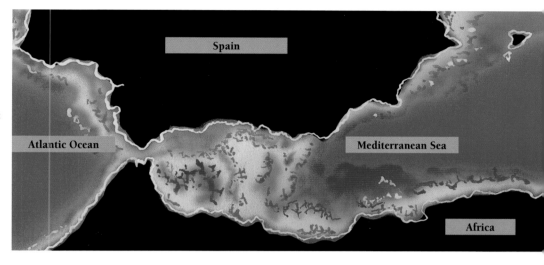

Spain

Atlantic Ocean

Mediterranean Sea

Africa

water is heavy and sinks to the bottom. A deep salty current flows into the Atlantic Ocean through the Strait of Gibraltar (above), while a less salty current flows across the surface back into the Mediterranean.

Ships' navigators must know about ocean currents,

and currents are also important to people who fish. In some areas, cold water from deep currents rises to the surface. This cold water is rich in nutrients that attract huge shoals of fish, which is why such areas are rich fishing grounds.

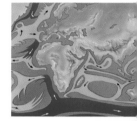

Ocean currents affect the climate of surrounding lands and bring warmth to some coasts and chill to others.

LIFE IN THE OCEANS

Scientists believe that life began in the oceans and that all living things on land are descended from sea creatures that, long ago, abandoned the sea and colonized the land. The creatures that stayed in the sea also evolved into millions of species. Each successful species developed its own way to ensure its survival.

Life in the oceans, like life on land, depends on the sun. Sunlight does not penetrate far below the surface, so the plants that use its energy live in the surface waters. Like green plants on land, they make their food by the process of photosynthesis, but unlike land plants, they are mostly microscopic. Many of them are single celled. Billions of these delicate plants float together in huge masses, along with slightly larger floating animals. Together, these microscopic organisms are called plankton.

A seabird, one of many creatures that find abundant food in oceans that teem with living things, snatches a fish from the waves.

Phytoplankton (greatly magnified)

Zooplankton (greatly magnified)

Plankton is the basis of the ocean food web (below). The plants (phytoplankton) are eaten by the animals (zooplankton), which are mostly larvae and little shrimp-like creatures. Both are eaten by mollusks, crustaceans, and fish, which are then eaten by larger fish, birds, and sea mammals such as seals and whales. Scraps of dead organisms sink to the bottom. Creatures that live on the seabed eat some of the scraps, while bacteria breaks down the rest and releases nutrients into the water that are carried to the surface by cold currents.

The open sea does not contain places for animals

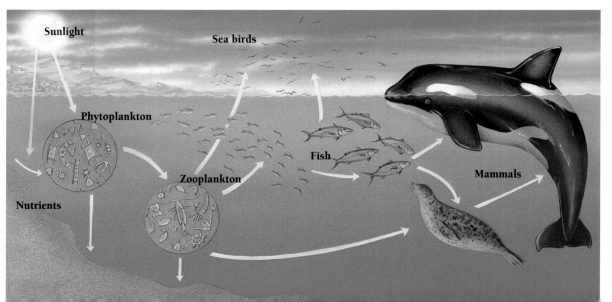

Sunlight

Sea birds

Phytoplankton

Fish

Mammals

Zooplankton

Nutrients

to hide. As a result, fish that feed on plankton usually swim in large groups, called shoals or schools (right). Massed together, they may deter predators by giving the confusing impression of being a single large animal rather than many individuals. Even if predators eat some of them, enough young fish will survive to breed and produce new generations of the species.

Ocean predators are well adapted to the task of catching their prey. The great barracuda (right) is the "tiger of the oceans." It has viciously sharp teeth and a sleek streamlined body that enables it to move swiftly through the water.

Reptiles and mammals are not as well adapted to sea life. Although turtles and seals (below) are excellent swimmers, both must come to the surface for air.

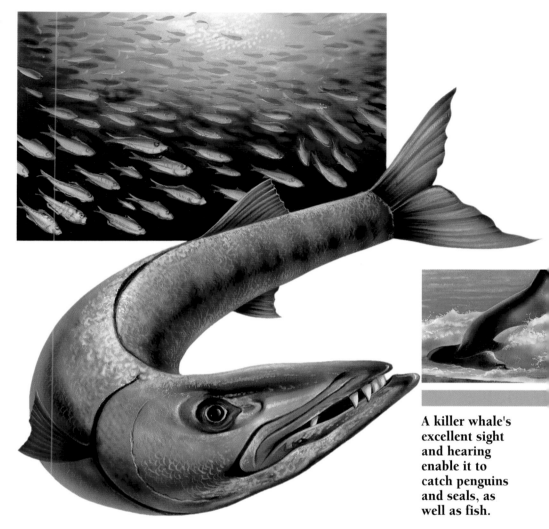

A killer whale's excellent sight and hearing enable it to catch penguins and seals, as well as fish.

The tiny plankton plants on which ocean creatures graze belong to a group of plants called algae. Seaweeds are also algae, but they are much larger. They grow on the seabed or float on the water around coasts to provide food and protection for animals that live close to the shore. Many small fish and other creatures live among the weeds, and larger ones come to prey on them.

SURVIVAL IN THE OCEANS

Sea creatures have a seemingly endless variety of shapes and colors, all of which have evolved to help them survive. Speed is essential for animals that have to pursue or be pursued by others, and a sleek streamlined shape is best for swimming. The tuna (top right) can reach speeds of up to 62 miles per hour (100 km/h).

Camouflage also helps animals to avoid detection. Flatfishes, including the flounder (above right), live on the seabed. As they move from place to place, they change their mottled colors to match the mud or sand below.

Fish that live near the surface, such as mackerel (right), are usually light in color on the underside and dark on top. A predator looking up from below will have trouble spotting the shimmering fish against the light shining through the surface, while a predator looking down will find it hard to make out the dark shape against the ocean depths.

These tropical fish (right) live in coral reefs and can change to really bright colors. Unlike the harmless flatfish of cooler seas, they are predators. Their camouflage enables them to watch and wait for their prey without being seen.

Sharks are the most feared of fish, although most do

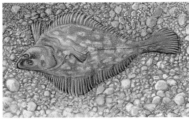

not attack humans, and some, such as the dogfish, are less than 40 inches (1 m) in length. The whale shark is the largest of all fish at 49.2 feet (15 m) or more. The fiercest sharks, those that have been known to harm people, are the white shark, the leopard shark, the tiger shark, and the blue shark. All have rows of sharp teeth in a large mouth on the underside of the head.

Many creatures that live on the seabed have evolved colors and shapes that allow them to merge into the background. This well-camouflaged fish could easily be mistaken for a stone.

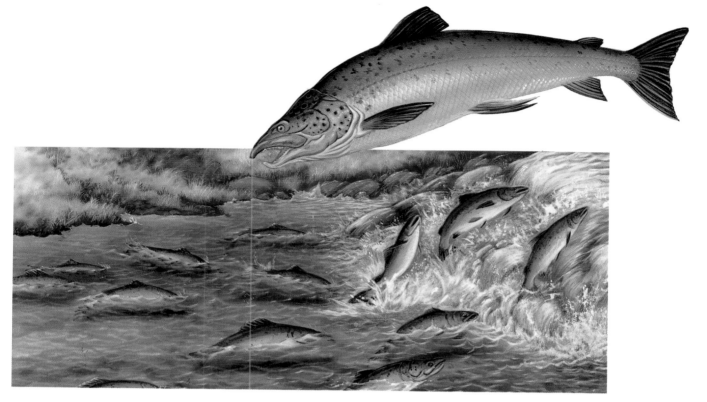

Some fish are great travelers. Salmon (above) start life as eggs that are laid in inland streams. The young fish stay in the river for about two years. Then they swim downstream to the sea and gradually mature into adult fish. Then, one day, they begin a journey back to the very place where they were born. This journey is more difficult, because the fish must battle their way upriver and even leap waterfalls. On reaching their birthplace, they breed, lay their eggs, and usually die.

Eels (below left) also make long journeys. They breed in a part of the Atlantic called the Sargasso Sea. Ocean currents carry the newly hatched fish toward the land. During the journey, the larvae turn into elvers (bottom). The elvers swim into a river and remain there for about ten years, before they migrate back to the Sargasso Sea to spawn. Most of those that survive the journey die soon afterward.

Some seabirds also migrate. Every year the Arctic tern (below right) breeds on Arctic coasts and then flies south to Antarctica and back again, which makes a round trip of more than 21,700 miles (35,000 km). The birds follow currents that encourage the growth of plankton and, therefore, the fish that the birds feed on.

Some fish and birds migrate to breed or to find food and make journeys that last years. Others move far shorter distances.

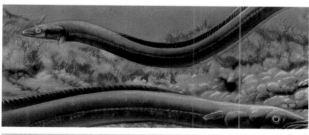

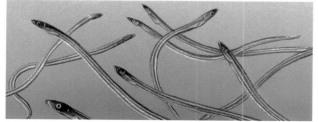

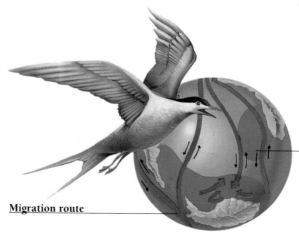

Winter areas

Migration route

17

IN THE DARK DEPTHS

Scientists once thought that animals could not live more than 197 feet (600 m) below the surface. But when researchers descended to the ocean depths, they found an assortment of fish and other creatures. The deeper they went, the stranger the animals became. At great depths, the water pressure is extremely high, temperatures are extremely low, currents move very slowly, and there is no light.

Without sunlight, plants cannot live, so deep-sea creatures must live on debris that floats down from above—or on each other. The fish mostly have huge mouths with razor-sharp teeth (top left). Some have elastic stomachs so that they can eat as much as possible when the opportunity arises. Some anglerfish have a lure attached to their heads (top right) that attracts prey.

Except at great depths, deep-sea fish are small with sensitive eyes, and nearly all of them produce their own light. Each species, like the viperfish (right), has a characteristic pattern of lights. The lights enable the fish to find food, recognize their own species, attract a mate, and scare away predators. Food is too scarce for fish to waste energy in pursuit of each other. They prefer to lie in wait for their prey. The deep-sea anglerfish (right) has a lure over its

head that it can switch on and off.

Creatures that live in the deepest parts of the oceans, below 9,843 feet (3,000 m), have virtually no color. Among them are worms, sea cucumbers, lampshells, and various crustaceans. They have little energy, so they move about rarely and slowly. Some bury themselves in the ooze. They get their nourishment from animal remains or droppings.

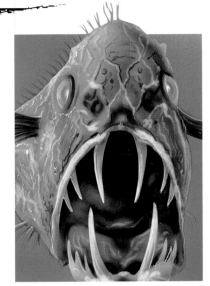

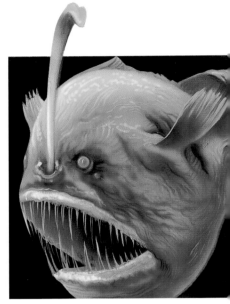

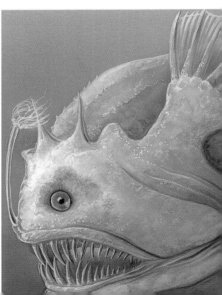

The tripod fish is one of many strange-looking deep-sea fish. Its extra-long fins and tail are stiff enough for it to stand clear of the muddy bottom while it waits for its prey.

In 1977, as scientists studied the ocean floor near the Galapagos Islands in the Pacific Ocean, they made an amazing discovery that was unlike anything else on the seabed. It was a vent (hole), through which hot water was rising. Around the vent was a "chimney" made of minerals such as iron, zinc, and copper that the hot water had contained. The scientists named the vents "black smokers," after the dark color of the water. More black smokers have since been found along the ocean ridges, where hot molten rock rises to the surface.

Black smokers form when water seeps down through cracks in the ocean floor (above). As it descends, the cold water is heated by the molten magma below. The water reaches temperatures of 1112°F (600°C) and becomes cloudy as minerals from the rocks dissolve.

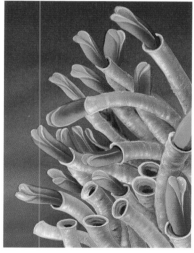

Finally, when it becomes too hot, the water shoots up through the vent and creates "islands" of hot water in the cold ocean depths.

Close to these warm spots, the scientists found some previously unknown creatures and bacteria that use minerals in the hot water to grow. The bacteria form the basis of the food chain for other creatures (above) that live around the vents. Among the strange creatures are giant tubeworms (left) that are up to 3.3 feet (1 m) long and live in white tubes anchored to the ocean floor. Other creatures include sea anemones, white crabs, blind shrimp, and clams the size of dinner plates (bottom left).

Although black smokers cannot support plant life because of the absence of sunlight, it may have been in conditions like this that life first began.

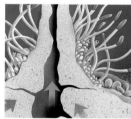

This cross-section view of a black smoker shows how the superheated water, darkened by dissolved minerals, rises through the vent and the surrounding chimney.

CORAL REEFS

The delicate tangled twigs (right) look like the branches of plants sculpted in stone. They are not plants, however, but living organisms, called corals. Corals are mostly colonial animals that live in tropical seas. Millions of them live together and their abandoned skeletons build up into huge structures, called reefs or coral islands (below).

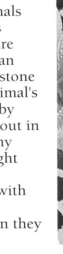

The individual animals are called coral polyps (right). Their bodies are soft and jellylike, but an outer skeleton of limestone protects them. The animal's mouth is surrounded by tentacles that wave about in the water and catch any tiny creatures that might bump into them. The tentacles are covered with poisonous stings that paralyze the prey when they touch it.

The shapes of corals are varied and beautiful. Some look like trees, some like domes, and some like organ pipes. Their bright colors fade if the living surface of the reef dies.

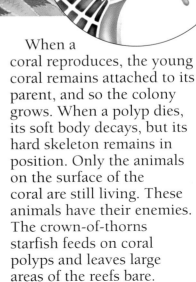

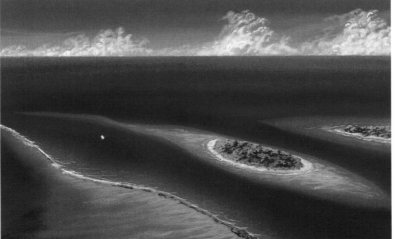

When a coral reproduces, the young coral remains attached to its parent, and so the colony grows. When a polyp dies, its soft body decays, but its hard skeleton remains in position. Only the animals on the surface of the coral are still living. These animals have their enemies. The crown-of-thorns starfish feeds on coral polyps and leaves large areas of the reefs bare.

Coral polyps thrive in warm tropical waters. The water must be clean and shallow. The polyps cannot live at depths of more than 197 feet (60 m), where there is not enough light. This is because they depend on tiny algae that live inside their bodies and use sunlight to make food, some of which goes to the polyps. The algae also supply chemicals that help to harden the coral skeletons. In return, the algae live in a protected place that is rich in mineral salts.

Coral reefs (top) are the home of great numbers of brightly colored fish, crustaceans, mollusks, sea anemones, starfish, and worms. Because reefs provide animals with protection and places to hide, they are major breeding grounds. Although coral reefs are hard, they are also fragile. Pollutants from factories and agriculture can easily destroy living colonies.

There are several kinds of reef. Fringing reefs are joined to the shore, while barrier reefs lie some distance from the shore. Atolls (below and left) are ring-shaped or horseshoe-shaped reefs that form around volcanic islands (1). As the sea level rises, or the island sinks, water fills the area (2). The coral thickens (3) and finally covers the volcano (4) and encloses the waters of the lagoon.

Colorful fish, like this angelfish, abound in coral reefs, where they can find plenty of food and hide from their enemies.

ICY OCEANS

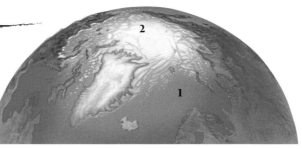
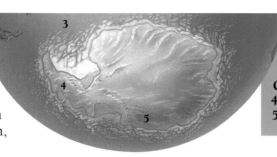

The coldest places on earth are at the poles (right). Around the North Pole is the Arctic Ocean, which is mostly covered by ice. The South Pole is covered by a huge frozen continent called Antarctica. The cold "southern ocean" that surrounds it is formed from the southern parts of the Pacific, Indian, and Atlantic Oceans.

1. Arctic Ocean
2. North Pole
3. Southern Ocean
4. Antarctica
5. South Pole

The Arctic Ocean is mostly covered by sea ice. The surface of the ice is rough because currents, tides, and winds make it fold into ridges.

The Arctic Ocean is largely enclosed by three continents: North America, Europe, and Asia. These landmasses do not allow warm currents to reach the area, which keeps the water in the Arctic Ocean cold. The sea ice that covers the ocean is formed from salty water. The Arctic also contains islands of ice formed from fresh water. These are icebergs that break away from ice caps and glaciers (left) that form over land areas.

Great layers of ice that vary in thickness cover Antarctica. On the coast, large ice shelves extend out from the buried land to jut over the sea. Occasionally, huge chunks of these great shelves break away and float in the sea as flat-topped icebergs (left). One of these icebergs in the Southern Ocean covered an area as big as Belgium.

The polar regions have a hostile climate that severely limits life on the land. No plants grow in Antarctica, except on sub-Antarctic islands, so only a few tiny insects and mites live there permanently. Most polar animals live on coasts or in the ocean. The ice-cold waters are rich in plankton, fish, whales, and dolphins, and the coasts are home to millions of seabirds, including penguins (top). Penguins live in the Antarctic. They hunt for fish in the sea but nest on land, and sometimes travel far across the ice to their breeding grounds.

The polar bear (center) lives in the Arctic. Its thick white coat makes the bear hard to see as it roams across the sea ice in its hunt for seals, which it sniffs out with its sensitive nose. Its warm fur and a thick layer of fat help it tolerate the extreme cold on the surface and in the water.

Polar seas are rich in planktonic creatures called krill (inset right). Krill are important food for whales, seals, seabirds, fish, and squids. The blue whale (right) is the largest animal on earth. It uses its baleen (sheets of horny material that hang from its upper jaw) to strain krill from the water. Krill are rich in protein. They could be-come a food for humans if an inexpensive way to harvest them could be found.

Harp seals are born with white coats, and their soft fur is prized by hunters. They are the most heavily hunted of all the world's seals.

OCEAN RESOURCES

People have used the oceans and their resources since ancient times. Seas were highways for early traders, such as the Phoenicians, who traded around the Mediterranean Sea more than 3,000 years ago. Even more ancient is the craft of fishing, which was practiced by the earliest humans and continues to be a major source of food all around the world.

Many families today get all their protein from fish caught in small boats with a crew of one or two people. Their methods leave plenty of fish in the sea to breed and produce new fish. Most of the world's fish, however, are caught by sophisticated ships (above right) that can haul in huge shoals in seine nets (center) that close around the fish and scoop them up. The biggest fishing ships, called factory ships, stay at sea for months and process, freeze, and pack the catch on board.

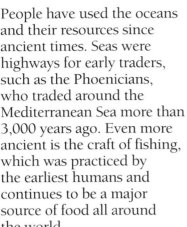

Mussels are farmed in many coastal areas, along with oysters, shrimp, and other kinds of shellfish.

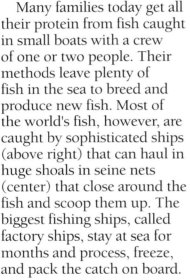

Modern fishing methods have led to overfishing in many areas. Even tiny fish are caught in the nets, and so none escape to breed and build up a new population. Some fish have disappeared from certain areas. As a result, international controls and fishing limits have been imposed to protect fish stocks. These have provoked conflicts between countries eager to protect their fishing industries.

One way to protect fish stocks is to raise fish on farms. These may be simple pools, netted cages, or sophisticated tanks (bottom), where the environment is completely controlled. The Chinese and Japanese have reared carp in ponds since ancient times and today lead the world in fish farming. Salmon and trout are bred on fish farms, as well as other sea products, such as seaweeds.

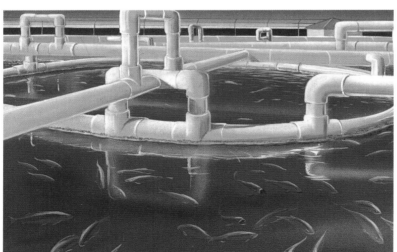

Other products that come from the sea, or beneath it, are oil, natural gas, gravel, sand, salt, and a variety of minerals. Gravel and sand are dredged from the ocean floor for use in building construction. Oil and gas are found in deposits in the rocks under the continental shelves. To reach the deposits, huge drilling rigs, which are mounted on offshore platforms (right), must dig wells. Some of

seawater. People dig shallow ponds, called pans, and flood them with seawater (center). The sun dries up the water and leaves the salt behind.

Seawater contains many dissolved minerals, such as gold. On the sea floor, there are nodules that contain manganese, cobalt, copper, iron, and nickel. The cost of

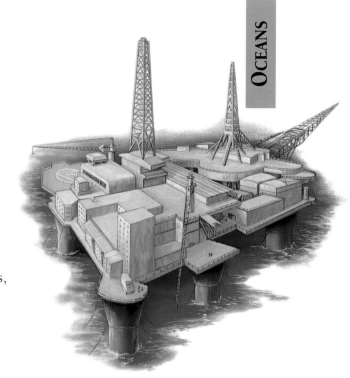

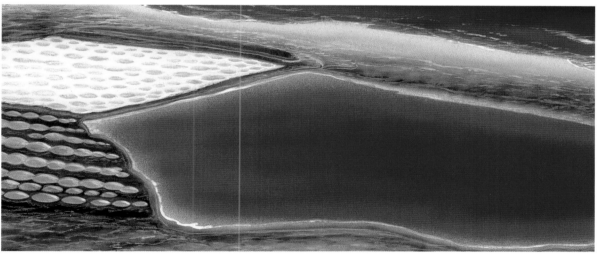

Oil rigs drill wells deep into the rocks under the ocean to reach deposits of oil trapped in the rocks.

these structures stand on the seabed, and others float, but all of them have to be immensely strong to withstand the battering of storms. The oil and gas are transported to land through pipelines or in large oil tankers.

Salt has been valued since ancient times. It is used to preserve food and enhance its flavor. On some coasts, traditional methods are still used to extract it from

extracting these minerals is high, however, and cheaper supplies still exist on land.

In some places, tides are strong enough to produce electricity. A dam is built across an estuary to hold back rising water. The twice-daily ebb and flow of the tide spins turbines in the dam (right) as the water flows in and out.

DAMAGING THE OCEANS

Because the oceans are so vast, people have always used them as garbage dumps. In some places, raw sewage and waste from coastal towns are piped out to sea (right). Factories dump dangerous waste chemicals into the water. Nuclear power stations pump contaminated waste into the water or dispose of radioactive waste in metal containers that they hope will last forever. Farmers pour fertilizers and pesticides onto the land, which later drains into rivers and ends up in the sea.

People have only recently become aware of the damage that all these poisons do to the delicate balance of sea life. These contaminants kill millions of sea creatures or infect their bodies and, in turn, poison the people who eat them.

Poisonous substances do not stay in the same place, because currents (center) move them around. Pollution in one area can spread to

A once beautiful beach is ruined by oil that has spread from an oil spill that may have occurred far away.

many other areas. All around the world, beaches are polluted and coastal waters made unfit for swimming.

Oil spills are common and lethal. Ships often deliberately release surplus oil into the water, and there are many accidental spills from tankers (bottom) and oil rigs. The oil spreads in a thick film, called a slick, over the surface. Sometimes a cargo of oil catches fire, and the surface of the sea is ignited.

Poisons from spilled oil sink into the water and kill undersea life. On the surface, seabirds become trapped in the thick oil. As they struggle to release themselves, they become exhausted and die. Thousands of seabirds have died this way. Even those that are rescued (right) may not survive. People clean the birds up, but they cannot replace the natural oil that protects the birds' feathers and makes them waterproof. Without this natural oil, the birds quickly die of cold.

The sea is very bountiful. It provides people with fish and many other benefits. But people have been careless with this resource. In many fishing grounds, fish that were once common, such as cod, have become rare. The overhunting of whales has brought some species close to extinction, and the hunting of some whales is now banned. Sea creatures, such as corals and shellfish, depend on clear clean water, but dredgers churn up the sea bottom and muddy the waters. People are now making efforts to cut pollution and to catch only mature fish (below). Nuclear dumping has been stopped, and greater safeguards against oil spills are built into the design of modern ships. In time, the seas and their wealth of wondrous wildlife may recover.

A sea turtle, covered in oil, lumbers ashore to die. The careless pollution of the oceans has endangered many sea species.

27

UNDERSTANDING THE OCEANS

TURNING WHITE

White sea foam occurs when waves break and air mixes with seawater. When you separate egg whites from the yolk and then beat the colorless egg whites (left), a similar process occurs. The circular movement of the fork mixes air into the egg whites, and the constant beating breaks the air into increasingly smaller bubbles. The end result is white foam, just like the foam along the seashore.

HOT AND COLD CURRENTS

Cold water is denser (heavier) than warm water, because the molecules in cold water are more closely packed together than they are in warm water. Therefore, warm ocean currents travel across the surface, while cold water tends to sink and travel at a lower level.

You can do an experiment to see this happen. First, partially fill a glass bowl with cold water. In another container, mix hot water with some red ink or food coloring. Then pour the hot colored water into the first bowl and see what happens. The colored water should float above the cold water.

MAKE YOUR OWN SALT

When seawater evaporates, the salt dissolved in it is left behind. You can see this happen if you fill a dish with water and dissolve plenty of salt in it. Leave the dish in a dry, warm place. Slowly, the water evaporates as molecules on the surface change from liquid into an invisible gas called water vapor that disappears into the air. The water level gradually falls until all the water has evaporated. Only crystals of salt are left on the bottom of the plate. If you examine the crystals through a microscope, you will see that they are mostly shaped like cubes.

LIGHTER THAN WATER

When water freezes, the molecules move apart and it expands. The ice that forms is less dense than the water. This explains why ice floats in water. It also explains why the layer of ice that covers the Arctic Ocean floats on the surface instead of sinking to the bottom. Huge icebergs float just like the ice cubes in a glass of water.

GLOSSARY

ABYSS The ocean depths, below the continental slope.

ALGAE Simple plants that range from microscopic one-celled phytoplankton to large seaweeds.

ATOLL Ring-shaped coral reef that encloses a lagoon.

AXIS Imaginary line around which the earth spins.

BACTERIA Microscopic organisms that occur everywhere in nature.

BASIN Depression in the earth's crust filled by an ocean or a sea.

CANYON A deep valley.

CLIMATE The typical or average weather at any place on earth.

CONDENSATION The process by which a gas changes to a liquid.

CONTINENT Large land area.

CONTINENTAL SHELF The gently sloping seabed around continents.

CONTINENTAL SLOPE The steep slope at the edge of the **CONTINENTAL SHELF** that leads down to the abyss.

CORAL Colonial animals that form reefs and coral islands.

CRUSTACEANS A group of animals with hard shells that includes crabs, shrimp, and woodlice.

CURRENT Stream of water.

DREDGING The removal of sediments and minerals from the sea bed by ships called dredgers.

EQUATOR An imaginary line that runs around the middle of the earth halfway between the poles.

ESTUARY The mouth of a river, where tides occur.

EVAPORATION The process by which a liquid becomes a gas.

FOOD CHAIN Sequence of organisms, in which each is a source of food for the next.

FOOD WEB The interaction of food chains.

GLACIER River of ice, formed from frozen and compacted snow, that moves downward.

GRAVITATIONAL PULL The force of attraction that acts between all objects.

guyot Submerged flat-topped peak.

HEMISPHERE Half a sphere; used to describe the north–south or east–west halves of the earth.

HYDROSPHERE All the water on earth.

ICEBERG Chunk of ice that floats in the sea.

ICE CAP Area of ice that covers the poles and the surrounding regions.

ICE SHELF A large area of ice attached to a mainland ice sheet that juts out over the sea.

LAKE An area of water entirely surrounded by land.

LARVAE The immature forms of certain animals that look quite different from the adults.

MICROSCOPIC Too small to be seen without the aid of a microscope.

MIGRATION The movement of animals or people from one area, or climatic region, to another.

MOLECULE The smallest unit of matter that retains the properties of the substance.

MOLLUSKS A group of soft-bodied animals that includes not only octopuses and squids but also clams, mussels, oysters, and snails (which have shells).

MOLTEN ROCK Fluid rocks inside the earth's mantle, also called magma.

NATURAL GAS Fuel found in rocks, often with or near deposits of oil. It was formed from the remains of once-living organisms.

NEAP TIDE Tides that occur twice a month, when the sun and moon pull at right angles to each other.

NUTRIENT Any nourishing substance.

OIL Fuel found in rocks, also called petroleum. It was formed from the remains of once-living organisms.

OOZES Sediments on the seabed that consist of various mixtures of mud, clay, and the remains of dead sea creatures.

ORGANISM Any plant, animal, or other living thing.

OXYGEN A life-supporting gas present in the air and in water.

OZONE A form of oxygen that forms a layer in the atmosphere and blocks out most of the sun's harmful ultraviolet rays.

PANGAEA The name given to the supercontinent that existed in prehistoric times and then split up.

PHOTOSYNTHESIS The process by which plants make food using sunlight, water, and carbon dioxide.

PHYTOPLANKTON See plankton.

PLANKTON Masses of small and often microscopic organisms that live near the surface of oceans and lakes and consist of **PHYTOPLANKTON** (simple plants) and zooplankton (animals).

PLATES Large slabs of the earth's hard outer layers.

POLAR REGIONS Two ice-cold areas; one is between the North Pole and the Arctic circle, while the other is between the South Pole and the Antarctic circle.

POLES The points, north and south, that mark the ends of the earth's axis.

POLLUTION Contamination of the land, air, or sea, usually with chemical or industrial wastes.

PROTEIN One of the types of food needed by the body to provide energy.

REEF Ridge of rock, sand, shingle, or coral that lies just under or on the surface of the water.

RIDGE Chain of underwater mountains formed when two plates move apart.

RIFT VALLEY A valley formed when a block of land sinks down between long faults (cracks) in the earth's crust.

ROTATION The spinning of the earth on its own axis.

salinity Saltiness.

SALT A chemical substance that gives seawater its taste.

SEDIMENT Worn fragments of rock, which includes sand, silt, and mud.

SIRENS Sea nymphs—part woman, part bird—in Greek myths, whose beautiful songs lured sailors to their death.

SPRING TIDE Tides that occur twice a month, when the sun and moon are pulling in the same direction.

TIDAL WAVE Term wrongly used to describe tsunamis and large waves that devastate coasts.

TRANSPIRATION The process by which the leaves of a plant give off water.

TRENCH Long, deep depression in the ocean, formed where two plates collide and one plate is dragged down beneath the other.

TROPICS The region between the tropic of Cancer and the tropic of Capricorn, two imaginary lines north and south of the equator. It is the world's hottest zone.

TSUNAMI Huge surge of water caused by underwater earthquakes or volcanic eruptions.

TURBINE A motor in which a wheel or drum is driven by moving water, steam, gas, or winds.

ULTRAVIOLET RAYS An invisible and dangerous form of light that comes from the sun.

VOLCANIC ISLAND An ocean volcano that has grown above the surface.

VOLCANO A hole in the ground from which molten rock (lava), steam, and gas escape, or a mountain formed by hardened lava or ash ejected from the hole.

WATER CYCLE The continuous process by which water evaporates from the sea, falls as rain on the land, and flows back from the land to the sea.

WATER VAPOR Water that has turned into an invisible gas in the air.

WHIRLPOOL Rapid circular movement of water.

WIND BELTS Bands of winds that circle the globe and blow in the same direction.

ZOOPLANKTON See plankton.

INDEX